BABY ANIMALS

Andrew Brown

 CRABTREE
Publishing Company

CRABTREE
Publishing Company

350 Fifth Avenue
Suite 3308
New York, NY 10118

360 York Road, R.R.4
Niagara-on-the-Lake
Ontario L0S 1J0

73 Lime Walk
Headington, Oxford
England OX3 7AD

Editor **Bobbie Kalman**
Assistant Editor **Petrina Gentile**
Designer **Melissa Stokes**

Illustrations by

Front cover: Mark Franklin (main), Wendy Bramwell/WLAA, Robin Budden/WLAA, John Cox/WLAA, Simon Turvey/WLAA;
Back cover: Evi Antoniou

Evi Antoniou (p. 8–9, 14–15), Wendy Bramwell/WLAA (p. 10–11), Robin Budden/WLAA (p. 12–13), John Cox/WLAA (p. 24),
Mark Franklin (p. 18–19), Tony Hargreaves (p. 20–21), Matthew Hillier/WLAA (p. 26–27), Carol Roberts (p. 16–17),
Valérie Stetten (p. 28–29), Kim Thompson (p. 6–7, 30–31), Chris Turnbull/WLAA (p. 25), Simon Turvey/WLAA (p. 22–23)

Created by
Marshall Cavendish Books, London
(a division of Marshall Cavendish Partworks Ltd.)
119 Wardour Street, London, W1V 3TD, England

First printed 1997
Copyright © 1997 Marshall Cavendish Ltd.

Cataloging-in-Publication Data

Brown, Andrew, 1972-
Baby animals
(Extraordinary animals series)
Includes index.
ISBN 0-86505-559-9 (bound)   ISBN 0-86505-567-X (pbk.)
1. Animals - Infancy – Juvenile literature.
2. Parental behavior in animals – Juvenile literature.
I. Title.   II. Series: Brown, Andrew, 1972-   .   Extraordinary animals series.
QL763.B76 1997   j591.3'9   LC 96-47204

Printed and bound in Malaysia

CONTENTS

INTRODUCTION

Baby animals are born in many different ways. Some babies, including humans, grow inside their mother's body. Other babies grow in pouches on their mother's body. Some babies, such as birds, reptiles, and fish, grow inside eggs.

MOTHERS

often stay near their newborn babies. The gray whale below carries her baby until it can swim on its own.

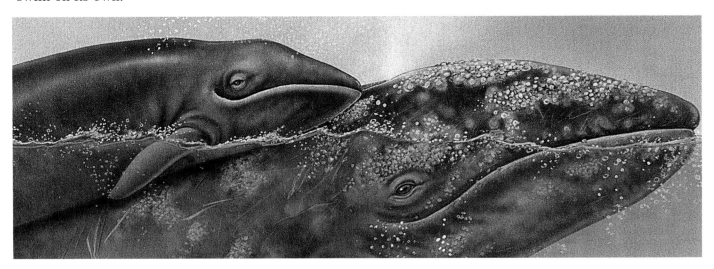

BABY FROGS

begin their lives in eggs. The mother lays the eggs underwater. Food inside the eggs helps the baby grow.

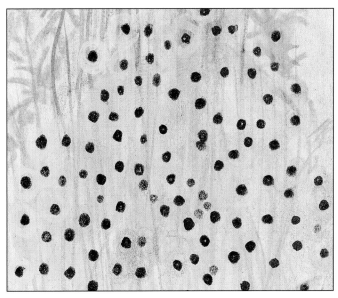

THE KANGAROO

is one of the smallest baby animals at birth. The baby quickly grows inside its mother's pouch.

ELEPHANT BABIES

grow inside their mothers' bodies longer than any other type of animal— almost 22 months!

KANGAROOS

Kangaroos are the largest type of marsupial. Female marsupials have a pouch on their stomach for carrying their babies.

Female kangaroos give birth to one baby, or joey. When it is born, the joey is tiny. It is only one inch (2.5 cm) long and weighs less than half an ounce (14 grams)! The joey has no hair and cannot see when it is born. It stays in its mother's pouch and drinks her milk for several months.

THE JOEY ◀◀◀

spends several months in its mother's pouch. After it leaves the safety of her pouch, the joey stays very close to its mother for a long time.

THE JOEY ▶▶▶

drinks its mother's milk
for almost 18 months.
Then the joey begins
eating grass.

JOEY ACROBATICS

The female kangaroo often helps
her young joey climb back into
the pouch. (1) The joey reaches
up with its paws and dives
into the pouch headfirst. (2)
The joey does a full
somersault and brings its head
back to the pouch opening. (3)
Once inside, only the joey's
head, paws, and tail can
be seen.

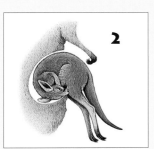

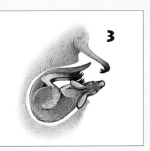

KOALAS

The koala is another kind of marsupial. Most female koalas give birth to one baby every two years. Newborn koalas are like baby kangaroos. They crawl into their mother's pouch. The female koala's pouch, however, opens at the bottom instead of at the top as with other marsupials. When it is inside the pouch, the baby koala feeds on its mother's milk. The baby stays in the pouch for at least five months.

After about eight months, the baby koala leaves its mother's pouch. Then the baby rides on its mother's back, clinging to her fur.

The baby koala eats eucalyptus leaves. The leaves help the koala grow. It could not survive without eucalyptus leaves.

◄◄◄ KOALAS
usually like to eat and sleep alone, but when a mother is nursing her baby, she carries it around on her back.

◄◄◄
EUCALYPTUS
leaves are the only food the adult koala eats. The leaves have lots of oil in them, which gives the koala all the liquid it needs.

GALAGOS

The galago lives in the African jungle. It can jump great distances from one tree to another.

When the female galago is about to give birth, she hides from the male because he might kill her babies. The female usually gives birth to one or two babies. The babies are covered with soft fur. During the day, the babies spend most of their time sleeping.

After a few days, the babies can grip tightly. They go out with their mother when she hunts for food. After ten days, the young can climb, stand, jump, and wrestle. The mother still carries her babies with her. By eight weeks, the galagos can look for food by themselves. They are fully grown at four months.

THE EYES ▶▶▶

are large and round. During the day, the eye is just a tiny slit. At night, it widens so that the galago can see in the dark.

▼▼▼ THE GALAGO
is sometimes called the
"bush baby" because its
call sounds like the cries
of a human baby.

◄◄◄ THE TAIL
is soft and thick. It helps
the galago keep its balance
when leaping from tree
to tree.

BEAVERS

The North American beaver lives along remote, wooded rivers and lakes in Canada and the United States. It is a very skilled builder. With its sharp front teeth, the beaver cuts down trees to build dams. Within the dam, the beaver makes its home, which is called a lodge.

The female beaver gives birth to up to eight babies, or kits. The kits are covered with fur at birth.

LIVELY LITTER ▼▼▼
The kits are born in the safety of the lodge. Other members of the family bring the kits tree bark— the beaver's main food.

◄◄◄ THE KITS

The kits stay with their parents for almost two years. Then the young leave the lodge to find a new home.

Within a few hours, the kit can swim, but it does not always want to go into the water. Kits usually prefer to stay in the warm, cozy lodge. Sometimes the mother beaver will pick up her kits and throw them into the water! Waterproof fur protects a beaver when it swims.

▼▼▼ THE TAIL

is flat and scaly. When the beaver swims, it uses its tail to move forward.

FRUIT BATS

Fruit bats are the largest and most powerful of all bats. They live in the forests and jungles of Africa, Asia, and Australia. They live in very large family groups. Fruit bats eat flowers and small insects as well as fruit.

The baby fruit bat has small wings and well-developed thumbs that can grip tightly. When the mother looks for food, she carries her baby with her until it is too heavy. Then she leaves it on a branch. If the baby should fall, the mother uses her memory, eyesight, and hearing to find it. She can find her baby quickly, even if there are thousands of screaming infants nearby.

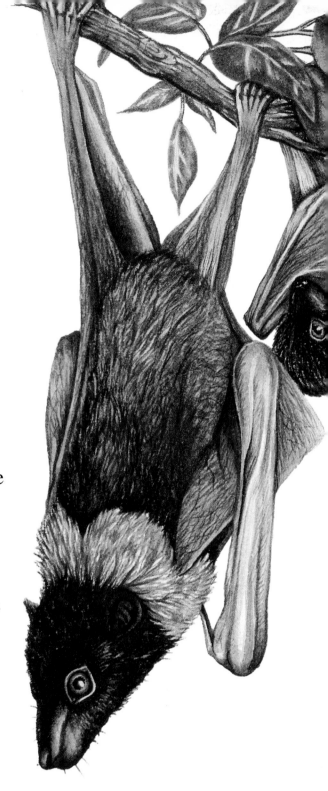

THE BABY ▶▶▶

fruit bat clings to its
mother's breast, even
when she looks for food.

◀◀◀ THE MOTHER

soon cannot carry her young
and gather food at the same
time. So she leaves her
babies on branches when
she gathers food.

FENNEC FOXES

Fennec foxes are very small foxes that live in the scorching hot deserts of North Africa.

A mother fennec fox gives birth to two to five cubs each year. Compared to other types of foxes, the fennec's litter has fewer cubs.

The male fennec brings food to the mother while she is nursing. Since the mother is very protective of her cubs, the male fennec leaves the food outside the den.

At nine months, the cubs are fully grown. The parents take care of the cubs for a long time. The fennec cubs practice their hunting skills by playing with one another. During the day, the fennec hides in cool sand burrows. At night, the fennec comes out to hunt for its favorite foods—small rats and mice.

▼▼▼ **THE FEMALE**

fennec is a fierce protector of her young. She may even attack the cubs' father if he comes too close.

▼▼▼ **THE FENNEC'S**

ears are very large. The fennec uses its excellent sense of sound to find prey.

BROWN BEARS

Brown bears live in more areas of the world than any other type of bear. They live in Asia, eastern Europe, and North America.

Female brown bears give birth to cubs during their winter sleep. Each fall, the female eats until it gets very fat and then falls asleep in the den. The den is either a hollow tree or a hole dug in the ground.

In the spring, brown bear cubs are born in the den. The cubs cannot see at birth. They are tiny and have no fur. The cubs stay in the den for the next few months, drinking their mother's rich milk. The milk is so healthy that the cubs grow very quickly.

THE CUBS ▶▶▶
are very playful. They love to stay near their mother.

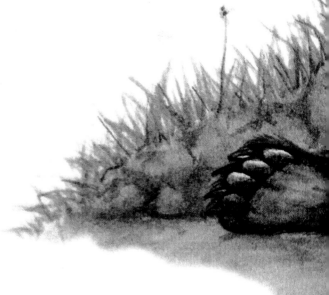

When the cubs come out of the den, their mother protects them. One of the most dangerous animals for the young cubs is the adult male brown bear because he sometimes eats cubs! If a mother bear thinks danger is nearby, she chases her cubs up a tree, where they will be safe.

◄◄◄ **THE MOTHER**
is very protective of her young.
She even guards them from
their powerful fathers.

PANDAS

Panda cubs are born in August and September. The female panda gives birth to two cubs, but one of them usually dies. Panda cubs are born blind. They have no teeth or fur. The mother stays with the cubs until they are about a year and a half. Then the cubs leave their mother and take care of themselves.

◄◄◄ THE MOTHER
stays in the safety of her den for the first month of her baby's life.

THE CUB ▶▶▶

can walk and climb onto its mother's back when it is six months old.

▼▼▼ BAMBOO

is a kind of large, tough grass. It is the panda's favorite food. The young cub eats bamboo when it is six months old.

CHEETAHS

The cheetah is the fastest land animal in the world. It can run as fast as a car. Cheetahs can hunt and kill prey very easily.

Before she gives birth, the female cheetah finds a nest to protect and shelter her newborn cubs. The nest is hidden in thick marsh or under bushes. At birth, the cubs are blind and helpless. They are covered with a soft, furry coat, which looks like bunches of dry grass.

◄◄◄ AT TWO WEEKS, cheetah cubs open their eyes. They also start to grow their spotted coat.

Sometimes there are as many as eight cubs in each litter, but only a few of them will survive. Most cheetah cubs die before they are three months old. Many are attacked by dangerous animals, such as lions. The cubs can also catch diseases very easily.

After three months, however, the cubs begin to grow strong. They learn to hunt, and soon they can kill hares and other small animals. When they are about a year old, the cheetahs are ready to leave their mother.

▲▲▲ **THE MOTHER**
looks for a new nest every couple of days. Since the nests attract bugs that can cause diseases, the mother moves and carries the cubs, one at a time, to their new home.

CHIMPS

Female chimps give birth to one or two young. Newborn chimpanzees are helpless, so they stay close to their mother. Baby chimps are very good imitators. They learn how to find food by watching the adult chimps in their groups. Some humans have even taught young chimps sign language!

THE BABY ▶▶▶ chimp rides on its mother's back when it is between five and seven months old.

CHIMPANZEES ▶▶▶ have very long arms and short legs. They walk using the soles of their feet and the knuckles on their hands.

THE MOTHER ▶▶▶

takes care of her young for a very long time. The baby chimp often stays with its mother for seven years!

ELEPHANTS

A long time ago, there were more than 350 kinds of elephants. Now there are only two—the African and the Asian.

The African elephant is the largest land animal on earth. The female also has the longest pregnancy period. After 22 months, it gives birth to one calf. The calf can normally stand after half an hour, but it needs several adults to look after it. Sometimes females in the herd watch each other's young. They protect the calves from hungry enemies, such as cheetahs and lions.

THE HERD ▶▶▶

is led by the oldest female of the group. She decides where the herd should travel, what the elephants should eat, and where they should rest.

ELEPHANTS ▶▶▶

are very sensitive to touch. From birth, a mother and her calf stay close. They love to stroke one another with their trunks.

Newborn calves drink their mother's milk. They also try to eat grass, but often it is too hard for the calf to pick up the blades of grass with its trunk.

Young elephants love to play. They charge at each other and bang their heads together. Playing helps young elephants improve their fighting skills.

FROGS

Frogs are amphibians. An amphibian is an animal that can live on land and in the water.

Female frogs lay thousands of tiny jelly-like eggs in the water. After a few days, the baby frogs, called tadpoles, begin to grow inside the eggs. They leave the eggs after ten days. Then they feed on weeds in the water. At first, the tadpoles have tails like fish. After three months, they have grown arms, legs, and lungs. The young frogs can now leave the water.

THE ADULT ▶▶▶
is fully grown after three years. It can live for more than ten years!

▼▼▼ FROGS

have short front legs.
The back legs are large
and strong for jumping
and swimming.

THE FROG'S EGGS

Frog eggs are covered with a jelly-like coating,
which protects them in the water. The baby
frogs, or tadpoles, can be seen inside. When
they leave the eggs, tadpoles have tails and gills,
which help them live under water. Slowly, they
turn into adult frogs that can live on land.

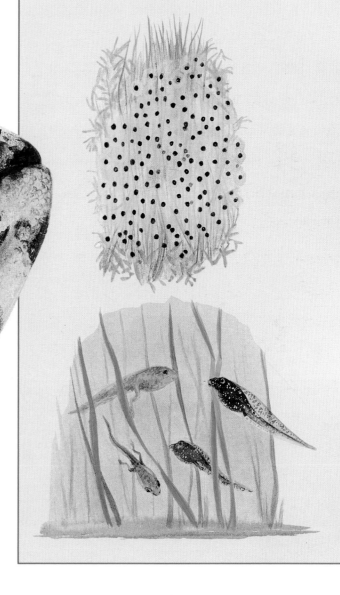

GRAY WHALES

Gray whales live in the north Pacific Ocean. Each year, they swim along the west coast of North America. In the summer, they live in the Arctic near Alaska. In the winter, they swim down to the warmer waters of California. Sometimes the whales swim very close to the shore.

The gray whale usually gives birth to one calf. It is born tailfirst in the warm water near California. At birth, the calf cannot swim very well. Sometimes the mother whale carries her calf up to the surface on her back, so it can take its first breath of air.

THE TAIL ▼▼▼
is over 9 feet (3 m) from tip to tip. It moves up and down to push the whale through the water.

▼▼▼ **THE CALF**
is smooth, sleek, and
glistening when it is born.

▼▼▼ **ADULT WHALES**
are covered with tiny
creatures called barnacles.
The barnacles form layers,
which become thicker as the
whale gets older.

The mother and calf stay in
the warm, shallow water until the
calf can swim properly. After about two
months, they start to swim north. When
they reach the Arctic, the calf develops
a thick layer of fat, called blubber, on its
body. Blubber keeps the whale warm in cold water.

During the summer, the calf grows very quickly. It gains two pounds
(1 kg) every hour! The female is usually larger than the male. Gray whales are
fully grown when they are 30 years old. Until then, they must be very careful.
Sharks and orcas often attack and eat young gray whales. Adult whales
sometimes have scars where they were attacked as youngsters.

INDEX

GLOSSARY

burrow – a hole dug in the ground by an animal for living or hiding

dam – a pile of wood or stones used to hold back water

eucalyptus – a type of evergreen tree or shrub which grows in warm places. Some animals, such as the koala, eat the leaves of this plant.

gill – the organ a fish and other water animals use to breath under water

herd – a group of animals, such as elephants or reindeer

litter – young animals born at the same time

lodge – a beaver's home

prey – an animal that is hunted by another animal for food

shark – a saltwater fish with a big mouth and several rows of sharp teeth